The All About Series

All About ... Canadian Attractions

Auyuittuq
National Park Reserve

Barb McDermott and Gail McKeown
Reidmore Books

Reidmore Books Inc.

For more information contact
Nelson Thomson Learning,
1120 Birchmount Road,
Scarborough, Ontario,
M1K 5G4.
Or you can visit our
internet site at
http://www.nelson.com

Printed and bound in Canada
2 3 4 5   03 02 01 00

We acknowledge the financial support of the
Government of Canada through the
Book Publishing Industry Development Program (BPIDP)
for our publishing activities.

Canada

Canadian Cataloguing in Publication Data
McDermott, Barb.
All about Canadian attractions : Auyuittuq National Park Reserve

(All about series)
Includes index.
ISBN 1-896132-35-9

1. Auyuittuq National Park Reserve (Nunavut)—Juvenile literature. I. McKeown, Gail.
II. Title. III. Series: McDermott, Barb. All about series.
FC4314.A88M32 1999   j971.9'5   C99-910580-9   F1105.A89M32 1999

About the Authors

Barb McDermott and Gail McKeown are highly experienced
kindergarten teachers living in Ontario. Both hold Bachelor of Arts and
Bachelor of Education degrees, Early Childhood diplomas, specialist
certificates in Primary Education, and have completed qualification
courses in Special Education. As well, Gail has a specialist certificate in
Reading and Visual Arts, and Barb has one in Guidance.

Credits

Editorial: Leah-Ann Lymer, Scott Woodley, David Strand,
Debbie Culbertson, Alice Blokland
Illustration, design and layout: Bruno Enderlin, Leslieanna Blackner Au
Maps: Wendy Johnson, Johnson Cartographics

Photo Credits

Cover photo: Summit Lake, by R.D. Muir/Auyuittuq National Park Reserve
Stamp photo: Woman in Sealskin, by Tessa Macintosh

Page

1 Mike Beedell
5 Tessa Macintosh
7 Auyuittuq National Park Reserve
9 G. Klassen/Auyuittuq National Park Reserve
11 Auyuittuq National Park Reserve
13 Auyuittuq National Park Reserve
15 R.D. Muir/Auyuittuq National Park Reserve
17 Auyuittuq National Park Reserve
19 Wayne Lynch
21 Wayne Lynch
23 Wayne Lynch
25 Mike Beedell
27 Mike Beedell

We have made every effort to identify and credit the sources of
all photographs, illustrations, and information used in this textbook.
Reidmore Books appreciates any further information or corrections;
acknowledgment will be given in subsequent editions.

Table of Contents
(All about what's in the book)

Introduction
(All about the beginning)

Auyuittuq National Park Reserve is a 1 970 000 hectare park with mountains, **glaciers, fiords,** and **valleys.**

The park is located in the **territory** of Nunavut.

The Inuit have lived in the park area for 1000s of years.

The park was created in 1976.

The park was made to **protect** the land, water, animals, and plants.

Auyuittuq National Park Reserve

Location
(All about where Auyuittuq National Park Reserve is in Canada)

Auyuittuq National Park Reserve is located in eastern Nunavut.

The park is located on the Cumberland **Peninsula** on Baffin Island.

The park is located beside Davis Strait.

People can enter the park by riding a boat or snowmobile from Pangnirtung or Broughton Island.

History
(All about how Auyuittuq National Park Reserve began)

The Inuit have lived on Baffin Island for 1000s of years.

In the past the Inuit lived by catching seals, walruses, and beluga whales.

Auyuittuq means "The Land That Never Melts" in the Inuit language of Inuktitut.

In 1585 John Davis became the 1st British person to explore Baffin Island.

People from Scotland came to hunt whales in the area in the 1800s.

Inuit Live on Baffin Island

Land
(All about the land in Auyuittuq National Park Reserve)

Auyuittuq National Park Reserve has the Penny **Highlands** in the middle of the park.

The Penny Highlands has mountains that are 2100 m high.

The Penny Highlands is covered with solid ice called the Penny Ice Cap.

The Penny Ice Cap is about 600 000 hectares in size and is 300 m thick.

The Penny Ice Cap may have been created in the last **Ice Age.**

The Penny Ice Cap

Land
(All about the land in Auyuittuq National Park Reserve)

Auyuittuq National Park Reserve has Akshayuk Pass.

Akshayuk Pass is a U-shaped valley carved through the mountains by glaciers.

Akshayuk Pass is 97 km long and is free of ice.

Akshayuk Pass is located between Cumberland Sound and Davis Strait.

Akshayuk Pass

Land
(All about the land in Auyuittuq National Park Reserve)

Auyuittuq National Park Reserve has Thor Peak.

Thor Peak is a mountain that is 1675 m high.

Thor Peak is named after the **Norse** god of thunder.

The **coastline** of the park has deep fiords with cliffs as high as 900 m.

The fiords were made by glaciers.

Thor Peak

Waterways
(All about the water in Auyuittuq National Park Reserve)

Auyuittuq National Park Reserve has Schwartzenbach Falls.

Schwartzenbach Falls is 660 m high.

Auyuittuq National Park Reserve has Summit Lake.

Summit Lake is located at the highest point of Akshayuk Pass.

Summit Lake's water flows through Weasel River and Owl River into the Arctic Ocean.

Summit Lake

Waterways
(All about the water in Auyuittuq National Park Reserve)

Auyuittuq National Park Reserve has Weasel River.

Weasel River is full of glacial milk.

Glacial milk is water filled with rock that has been crushed into fine bits by glaciers.

Crater Lake is located on the west side of Weasel River.

Crater Lake is greenish blue and is shaped like a circle.

Weasel River

15

Climate
(All about the weather in Auyuittuq National Park Reserve)

Auyuittuq National Park Reserve has long, cold winters.

The park has short, cool summers.

The park has almost no sunlight in the winter.

The park has many hours of sunlight in the summer.

The park has very little rainfall or snowfall.

Auyuittuq Has Cold Winters

Vegetation
(All about the plants in Auyuittuq National Park Reserve)

Auyuittuq National Park Reserve has **lichens,** mosses, and arctic willows.

The park has white mountain avens, yellow arctic poppies, and purple saxiflage.

The park has crowberries and bilberries.

The plants in the park grow in groups to keep warm.

Crowberries

19

Wildlife
(All about the animals in Auyuittuq National Park Reserve)

Auyuittuq National Park Reserve has lemmings, Arctic foxes, Arctic hares, wolves, polar bears, and caribou.

The park has walruses, ringed seals, harp seals, and bearded seals.

The park has narwhal, orca, beluga, bowhead, and humpback whales.

Walruses

Wildlife
(All about the animals in Auyuittuq National Park Reserve)

Auyuittuq National Park Reserve has over 35 kinds of birds.

The park has ptarmigans, snowy owls, eider ducks, ravens, glaucous gulls, and Canada geese.

The park has northern fulmars, thick-billed murres, and black guillemots.

The park has plovers, sandpipers, and American pipits.

The park has peregrine falcons and gyrfalcons.

A Gyrfalcon

Activities
(All about what to do in Auyuittuq National Park Reserve)

People come to Auyuittuq National Park Reserve to climb mountains, study the land, fish for arctic char, and hike.

Hikers must be able to look after themselves because the land can be difficult to cross, and the weather can change quickly.

Hikers need to know how to walk through streams that are high and flow quickly.

Hikers travelling across glaciers must wear **crampons** so that they do not slip and hurt themselves.

Hiking in Auyuittuq

Summary
(All about the ending)

Auyuittuq National Park Reserve has mountains, valleys, glaciers, and fiords.

The park has the Penny Ice Cap, Akshayuk Pass, Weasel River, and Thor Peak.

People who come to the park must know how to take good care of themselves.

Auyuittuq National Park Reserve is an amazing attraction ... found in Canada!

A Glacial River in Akshayuk Pass

Glossary

(All about what the words mean)

coastline (page 10)
A coastline is land along the edge of an ocean.

crampons (page 24)
Crampons are a set of spikes that hikers or climbers put on the bottom of their shoes. Crampons keep the hiker or climber from falling.

fiords (page 1)
Fiords are long, thin bays surrounded by high cliffs.

glaciers (page 1)
Glaciers are large sheets of ice. Glaciers move slowly and push dirt and rocks.

highlands (page 6)
Highlands are land with many mountains or hills.

Ice Age (page 6)
The Ice Age was a time when snow and ice covered most of the Earth.

lichens (page 18)
Lichen is a flowerless plant that grows on rocks and trees. Lichens are grey, yellow, brown, black, or green.

Norse (page 10)
The Norse people were from Norway and lived a long time ago.

peninsula (page 2)
A peninsula is a piece of land almost surrounded by water. Peninsulas stick far out into the water.

protect (page 1)
To protect something is to defend it from harm.

territory (page 1)
A territory is a region in Canada that has its own elected government. A territory, however, does not have the same powers as a province.

valleys (page 1)
A valley is land between hills or mountains.